The Brochs of Gurness and Midhowe

Noel Fojut
Principal Inspector of Ancient Monuments

Brochs are unique to Scotland. Although there are well over 500 of them, the majority spread throughout northern and western Scotland and the islands, there are few excavated examples that can provide a more vivid impression of life in the Iron Age than Gurness and Midhowe. Many of these tall towers stood alone, but in Orkney they were generally surrounded by sizeable villages, which can be seen at Gurness and Midhowe.

This booklet provides a guided tour to Gurness and Midhowe. But more than this it offers an insight into the nature of the society that built these settlements, the architecture of brochs and what it would have been like to live in Orkney 2000 or so years ago.

The Brochs of Eynhallow Sound

The Broch of Gurness with Eynhallow Sound and Rousay in the background.

Strung out along either side of Eynhallow Sound is a series of brochs: at least five on the shore of Rousay and six on the mainland coast. From Gurness on the mainland it is possible to look over the narrow and dangerous waters of the Sound to Midhowe on Rousay. This concentration of Iron-Age settlement reflects the convenience of locations beside the sea for transport and for food. It may be suggested that the shores of this strip of water represent the heart of Iron-Age Orkney, much as the ridge between the Lochs of Stenness and Harray, also on the mainland, represented the heart of Neolithic Orkney.

The sea has attacked the shoreline in the 2000 years since these brochs were built. A part of each settlement has been washed away and the coastline is still subject to erosion. The builders used stone from the shore, but what can be seen today alongside the sites are in fact modern concrete coastal defences.

Looking down on Midhowe Broch. (Copyright Richard Welsby.)

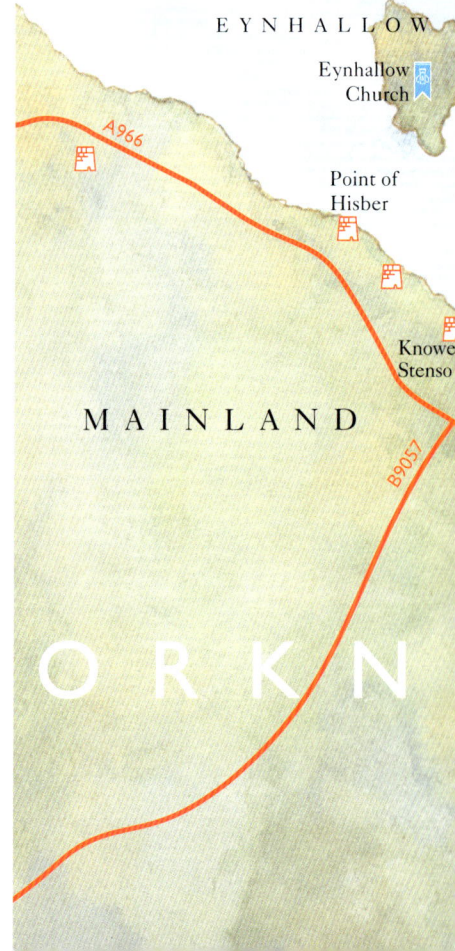

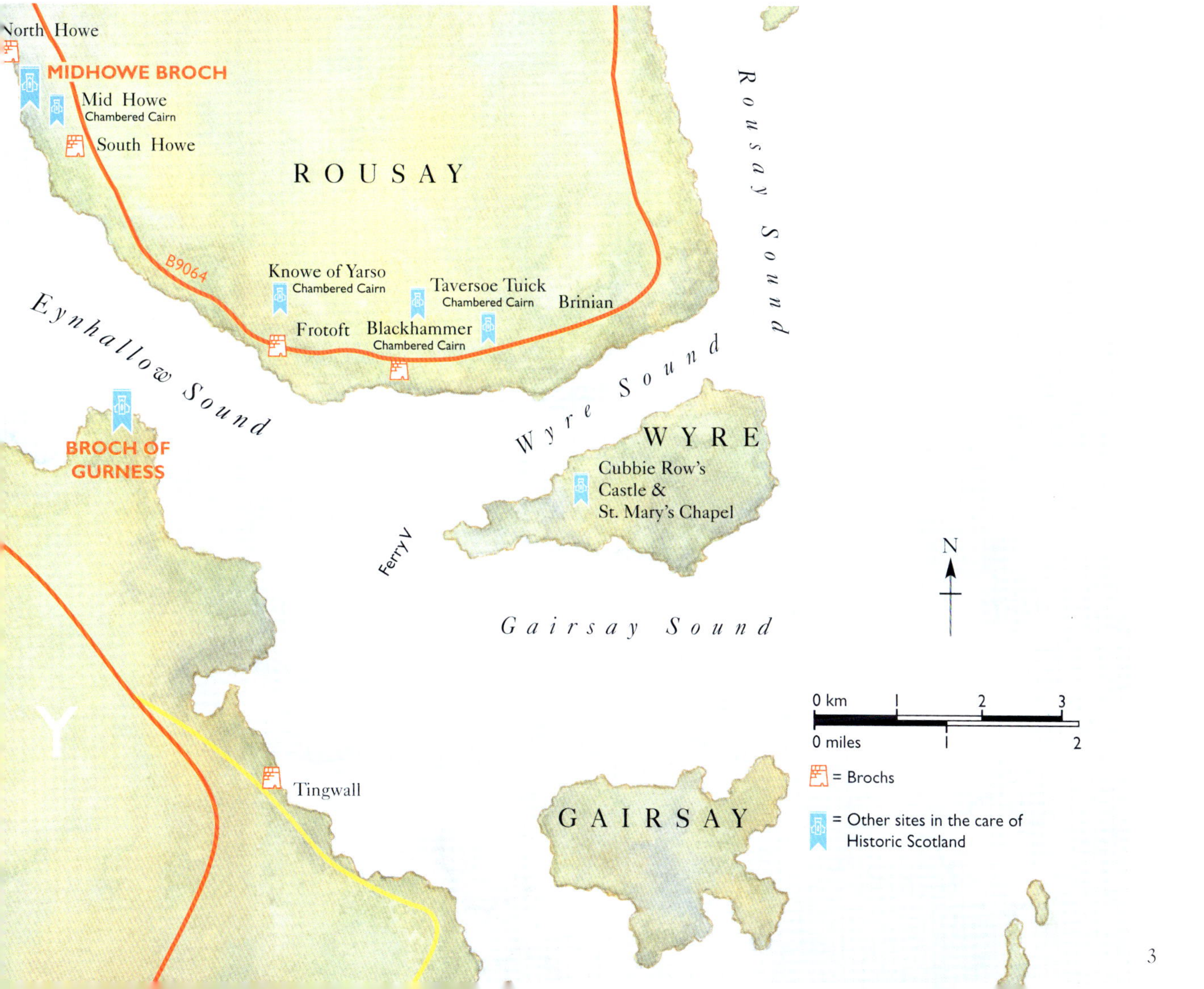

North Howe

MIDHOWE BROCH

Mid Howe
Chambered Cairn

South Howe

R O U S A Y

B9064

Knowe of Yarso
Chambered Cairn

Taversoe Tuick
Chambered Cairn

Brinian

Frotoft   Blackhammer
Chambered Cairn

E y n h a l l o w   S o u n d

W y r e   S o u n d

R o u s a y   S o u n d

**BROCH OF
GURNESS**

W Y R E

Cubbie Row's
Castle &
St. Mary's Chapel

Ferry V

G a i r s a y   S o u n d

N

0 km   1   2   3

0 miles   1   2

= Brochs

= Other sites in the care of
Historic Scotland

Tingwall

G A I R S A Y

The Broch of Gurness

Before excavation, Gurness was a large grass-covered mound on the edge of the peninsula of Aikerness. It was generally believed to be a broch, one of a group of such structures ranged along the shores of Eynhallow Sound. There was little to be seen apart from a central rise and a depression circling the site. These later proved to be, respectively, the broch tower and the outer defences. The sea had eroded part of the north side of the mound.

Excavation took place from 1929, and lasted for several years. The results were never fully published, and the account given here is based on a reassessment of the evidence made in the early 1980s, using the surviving records, the finds, and comparative evidence from recent excavations on other sites. Not all archaeologists agree with this suggested sequence of events.

At some date between 500 BC and 200 BC, probably nearer the latter, a decision was taken to create a new settlement at Gurness. A large area was marked out, approximately circular in plan and 45 m across. Around this were dug deep ditches with ramparts. There seems to have been a slight rampart on the inner side of the innermost ditch. On the platform so created there was probably a small settlement from the beginning, but all trace of this has been mostly lost below the subsequent remodelling of the site.

After a period of occupation, probably quite short, the ditches were cleaned out, relined and a new or rebuilt entrance causeway provided on the eastern side. Towards the western side of the enclosed platform work began on a circular broch tower, 20 m in external diameter and perhaps 8 to 10 m tall, while around it construction began on a settlement of small stone houses with attached yards and storage sheds. The broch had stone fittings on the floor, dividing it up into work areas and storage spaces, a single hearth and a deep 'well'.

Over the next few generations, the complex was modified, perhaps as part of an original plan. In the eastern part of the enclosure, structures began to be built out over the partially infilled ditch, which was relined once again, especially beside the entrance causeway. The broch tower fared badly, and a partial collapse on the western side necessitated a rebuild there, with buttressing. The internal arrangements of the broch were refitted, with new stone partitions, two hearths and the well being filled in and covered over.

Some time after AD 100, following a period of declining population and general disrepair, a further collapse led to the abandonment of the broch tower, the levelling of the surrounding settlement and the filling of the ditches. After this, the site seems to have been used for a succession of single farmsteads. One of these was found, partly dug down into the rubble, on the south-eastern part of the site. This house, known as the 'Shamrock', and a rectangular building, attributed to the Pictish or Viking period, were removed from the site and rebuilt to one side during the excavations.

The Pictish farm, too, was abandoned. The final archaeological evidence is a single Viking grave, placed on the by then deserted headland some time during the ninth century AD.

Gurness, before its excavation, was simply a large grassy mound beside the shore.

A Tour of Gurness

Five information viewpoints have been sited to guide you around Gurness. In addition, you will find a sixth on the shore to the west, near the carpark, from where you can look across Eynhallow Sound to Midhowe, on Rousay.

The Broch of Gurness from the air. (Copyright Richard Welsby.)

Visitor Centre

VIEWPOINTS

① *The 'Shamrock' House*

② *The Broch Ruins*

③ *The Village*

④ *The Entrance*

⑤ *The Broch Interior*

⑥ *The Shore*

1 The 'Shamrock' House

On the right, immediately opposite the Visitor Centre, is a small group of buildings which represent the latest construction on the site. They were moved to this location from the area to the south of the broch to allow excavation of underlying levels, and represent the best-preserved elements of a complex series of rather insubstantial building remains which were found in the mound during excavation. The main building is a small house, with a narrow entrance passage leading to a central room with a hearth. From this room four chambers open out, giving the four-lobed plan which has led to the house's popular name, the 'Shamrock'. The house was dug partly into the rubble of the earlier settlement, and would have had a low thatched roof, probably only tall enough to stand under at the centre of the main room. This diminutive building, of late Iron-Age or Pictish date, may give a measure of how far the status of the site had declined by the fourth or fifth century AD. Alongside it are reconstructed the walls of a sub-rectangular building, perhaps a byre for housing cattle.

A simple bone-handled knife from the Pictish levels. The marks on the handle may be ogham, an early form of writing.

This artist's impression captures life in the snug, dark interior of the 'Shamrock' House.

Gurness from the west, showing the massive foundation of the broch rising above a platform surrounded by deep ditches.

2 The Broch Ruins

Moving to the left, to the grassy strip outside the ditches, a good view of the ruins of the broch and surrounding settlement is obtained. The remains were excavated and consolidated as found, so the height of the surviving masonry is approximately what the excavators uncovered, although individual stones have been replaced and a good deal of mortar now holds together what was once entirely drystone walling.

The massive construction of the broch tower means that it has survived much better than the less robustly built houses which surround it. From this point, too, the scale of the surrounding ditches can be appreciated, together with the rather puzzling banks and changes in level which seem to be associated with later modifications to the site. The scale of the overall plan, and the size of the ditches, suggest that, if prestige was one reason for the construction of brochs, then Gurness was occupied by one of the most important (or self-important) families in Iron-Age Orkney.

Seen from above, the offset position of the broch and the interlocking outer foundations suggest a pre-planned layout.

3 The Village

Moving round the outer perimeter to the right, a good vantage point looks out over the complex of slight walls surrounding the broch tower. These are the remains of the village associated with the broch. There are six houses between the viewpoint and the broch. Each had an entrance opening from a passage running around outside the tower. Internally they had large living/sleeping rooms and smaller storerooms. Some had small yards open to the sky. Each living area had a hearth, a large tank set in the floor, cupboards and sleeping spaces. The houses would have been dark and smoky, with food stored hanging from the rafters away from vermin.

The village would have been noisy, smelly and an interesting place to live. In summer it would have been quiet during the day, as people worked on the shore or in the fields. During the winter it was probably crowded and claustrophobic, with everyone jostling for a well-lighted spot to work on bone tools, make straw ropes, prepare animal skins and thongs, spin or weave. Only the least domestic of activities, such as pottery manufacture, tanning hides or metalworking, would have taken place outdoors during the winter.

Upon closer examination, the tangle of walls on the platform outside the broch resolves itself into a series of small houses, each with at least one hearth. Each house has a small shed and access to an open yard.

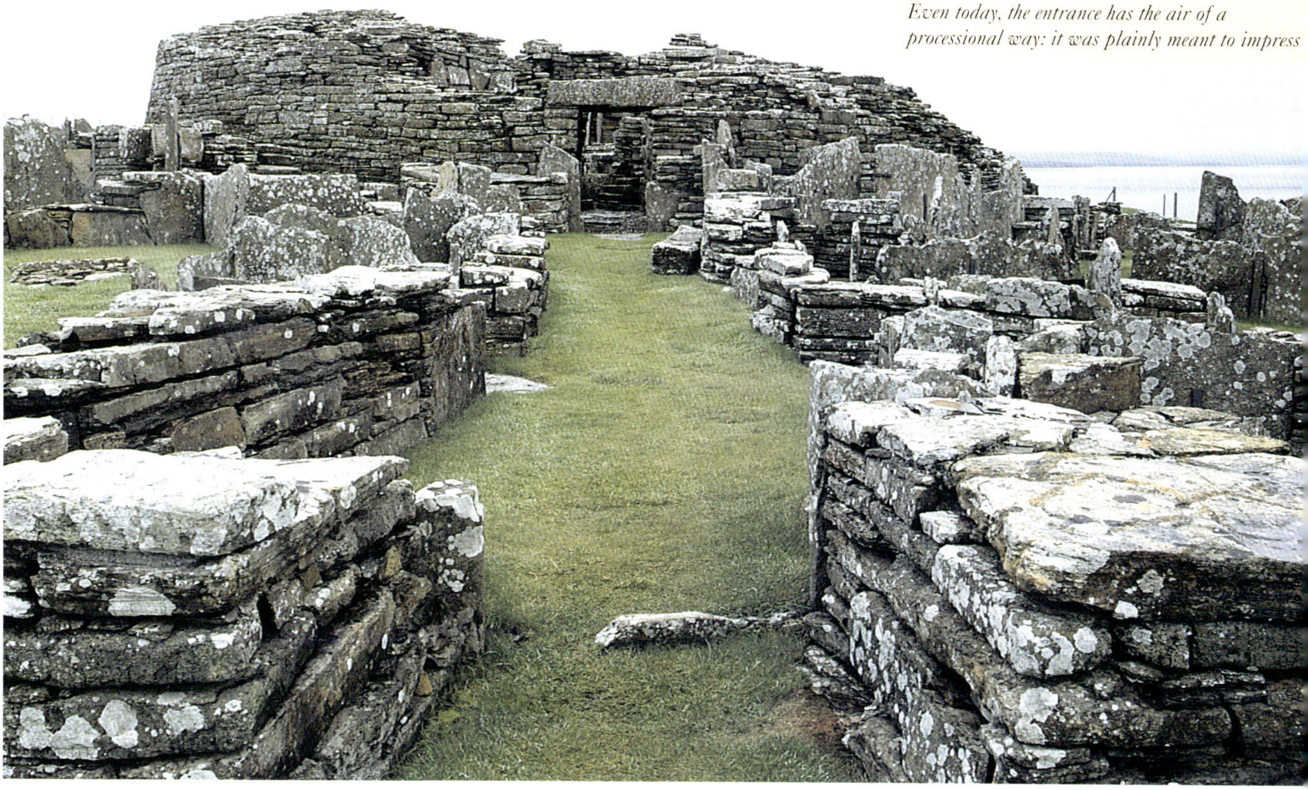

Even today, the entrance has the air of a processional way: it was plainly meant to impress

4 The Entrance

Moving onwards, the entrance comes into view. Behind the onlooker is the later Viking grave (see page 23).

The entrance area of Gurness is solidly built. A causeway leads across the outer defences, through two outer gateways. The visitor is now within the settlement, and a passage leads off left, giving access to the houses. To gain entrance to the broch two further doorways must be negotiated. One, added to the outside of the tower, has a low slab roof, but this dates only from the recent excavations. The second, the door proper, is deep within the entrance passage leading through the thick walls of the broch.

The doorway to the broch is flanked by upright stones, against which a wooden doorframe may have fitted. On the ground to the left is a pivot stone on which the door swung. Square holes in the passage wall housed a stout wooden bar, which could have been withdrawn from one of the cells on either side of the passage, within the wall thickness. Within the inner end of these rooms the distortion of the wall, caused by its partial collapse, may clearly be seen. This weakness required the hollow lower level of the wall to be packed with stone.

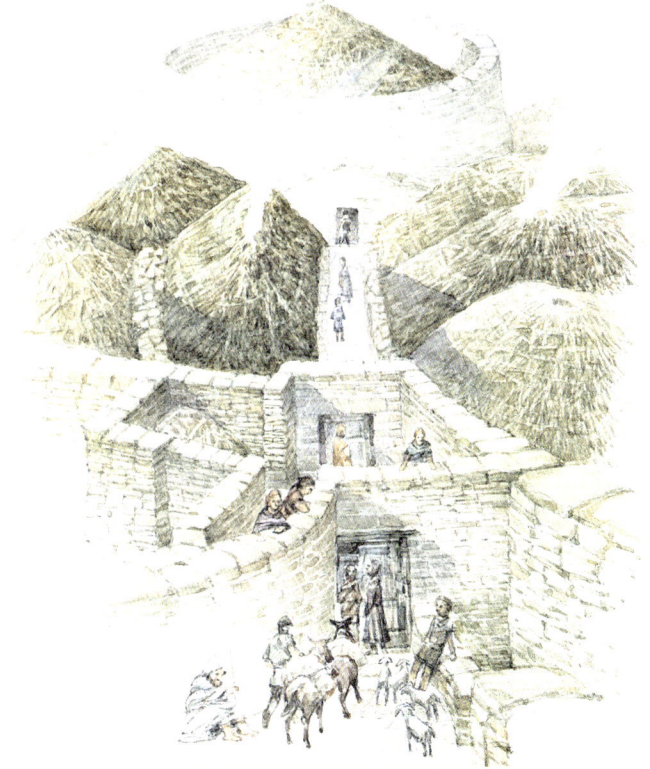

The artist's impression shows the arrival of a group of traders. Curious inhabitants, torn between alarm and interest, peer out as the visitors establish their credentials.

5 The Broch Interior

Originally the broch had a single central hearth, a 'well' and a ring of stone-built cupboards against the wall. After the partial collapse of the tower this arrangement was altered, and at the same time a new staircase was provided because the original was unsafe. (Several brochs collapsed around their stairs, suggesting this was a weak point in the broch design.) The 'well', if that is what it was, was filled in and the interior re-equipped with a new set of partitions. Most of what can be seen is from this second phase.

The view of the interior today is very partial, because only the stone fittings have survived. During the Iron Age the scene would have been very different. There may have been a raised wooden floor, the outer ends supported on the ledge or scarcement running around the inside of the wall. Over all would have been a conical, thatched, roof. Ladders would have supplemented the single stone stair. The thickness of broch walls, although a defensive feature, was also required to counterbalance the considerable outward thrust exerted by the internal structure and roof. An added bonus from these thick walls would have been protection from the winter winds.

Before leaving the site, wander outside the broch, down the little 'village street' into the smaller houses. Note how they are built into the ditch at several points. Also note the buttressing to strengthen the weak broch wall on the west side, and the way in which the western portion of the enclosed area has not been used, perhaps left clear for a development which was cancelled after the collapse of the broch on this side. It is worth remembering that Gurness is not fully excavated, and that there may be traces of earlier houses lying beneath those which are visible. These may hold the key to the question of what, if anything, preceded the broch village.

The interior floor of the broch would have been a busy place, with hearths, a 'well', storage pits and wall cupboards. Only fragments of this furniture survive today.

The 'Well' and its Parallels

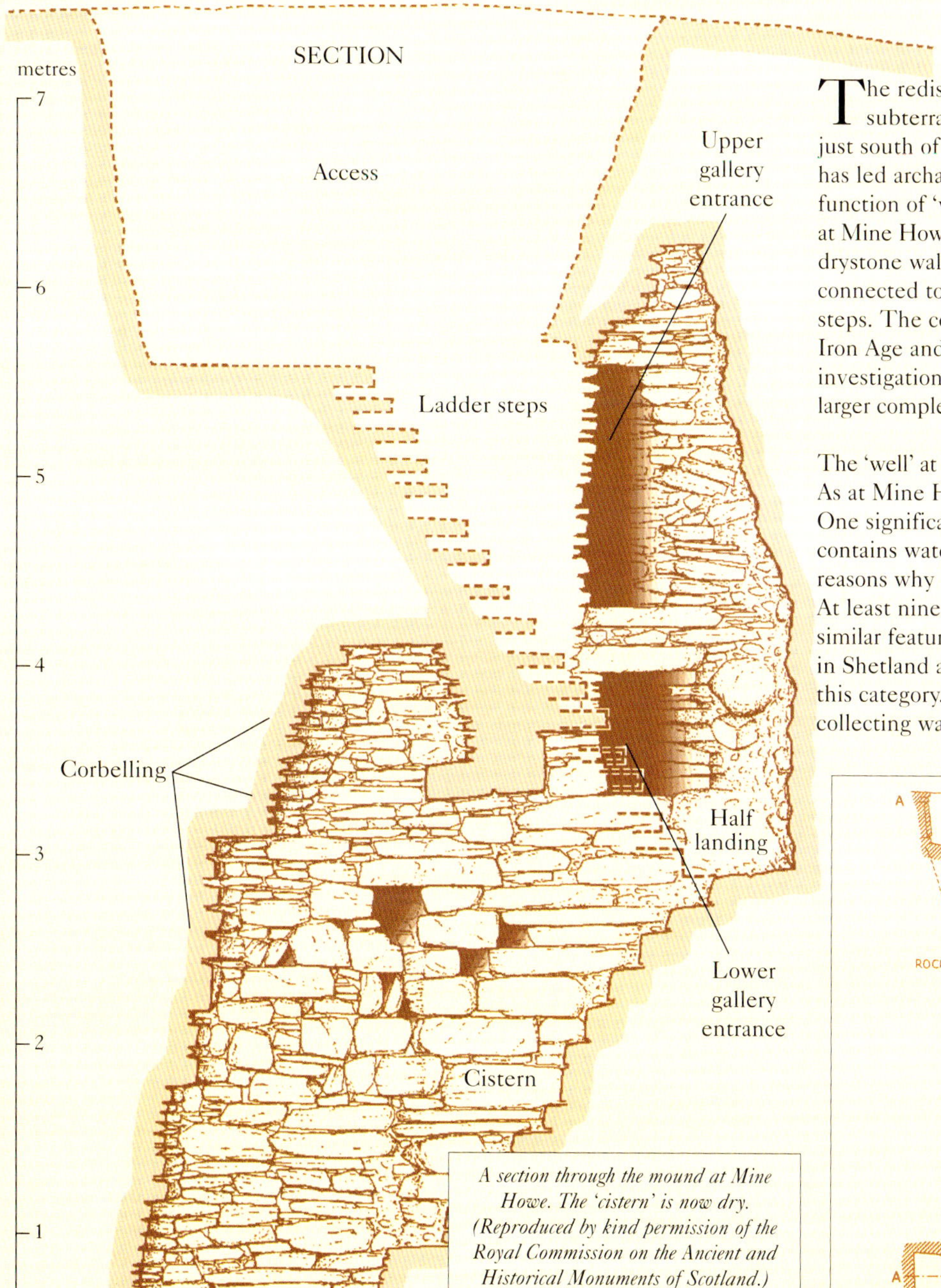

SECTION

metres

— 7

Access

— 6

Upper gallery entrance

Ladder steps

— 5

— 4

Corbelling

Half landing

— 3

Lower gallery entrance

— 2

Cistern

— 1

— 0.5

— section

A section through the mound at Mine Howe. The 'cistern' is now dry. (Reproduced by kind permission of the Royal Commission on the Ancient and Historical Monuments of Scotland.)

The rediscovery in 1999 of an extraordinary subterranean structure at Mine Howe, just south of the airport on Mainland Orkney, has led archaeologists to think again about the function of 'wells' within brochs. A large mound at Mine Howe contains an underground drystone walled chamber (7.4 m deep), connected to the surface by two flights of stone steps. The construction technique suggests it is Iron Age and preliminary archaeological investigation has shown it to be part of a far larger complex of remains, apparently ritual.

The 'well' at Gurness is in the broch interior. As at Mine Howe, it has associated chambers. One significant difference is that it still contains water (this and its steep steps are the reasons why it is not accessible to the public). At least nine other brochs in Orkney have similar features and there may be structures in Shetland and Caithness that also fall into this category. Was the Gurness 'well' just for collecting water?

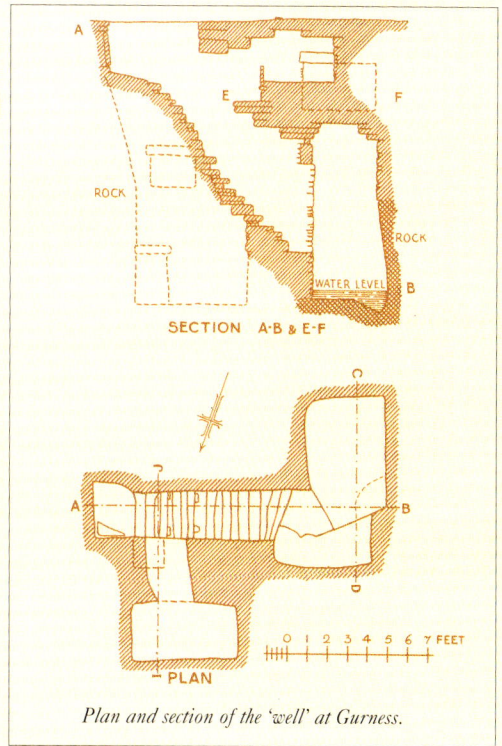

SECTION A-B & E-F

ROCK

ROCK

WATER LEVEL

PLAN

0 1 2 3 4 5 6 7 FEET

Plan and section of the 'well' at Gurness.

The Broch of Midhowe

The Iron-Age site at Midhowe was excavated in the same period as that at Gurness. Unlike Gurness, it has only a small settlement area additional to the broch, although some structures may have been lost to coastal erosion. Nearby are two other brochs, in ruins (hence the name, Midhowe = middle mound). Midhowe has features not present at Gurness, and it also produced a range of interesting artefacts indicating the extent of the contacts of the inhabitants.

During the latter centuries BC, the promontory on which the broch stands was cut off by two ditches, perhaps with an intervening rampart. The nature of the settlement within this earliest defence is not known. Subsequently, a massive stone wall was constructed immediately inside the outer ditch, and perhaps behind it a lean-to timber gallery. The inner ditch was partially infilled to allow this. Within the area thus enclosed a broch was built with a hollow wall extending from ground level. It has been suggested that this type of construction is early in the Orkney broch sequence, being later replaced by more stable solid-based brochs, but there is no dating evidence for this belief.

A complex of outer buildings was then constructed around the broch. These took a form similar to those at Gurness, with small houses, barns, byres and attached yards. Gradually these buildings were extended into the space formerly occupied by the wooden building behind the defensive wall. It is not known how much of the promontory has been lost to the sea, but it seems likely that the Midhowe village was never as extensive as that at Gurness. Also, there is some evidence that the Midhowe houses, unlike those at Gurness, are definitely later than the broch tower.

As at Gurness, the interior of the broch was filled with the remains of partitions and hearths, mostly dating to later phases in the use of the tower. Also as at Gurness, the tower collapsed partially at some date in the Iron Age, and was packed with stone within and buttressed without.

The massive wall, which is probably a stone-faced earthen rampart, with its resemblance to forts in Shetland (for example, Ness of Burgi) and to similar defences at Nybster in Caithness, is an interesting structure, but Midhowe's particular claim to archaeological importance is based on the artefactual evidence recovered during the excavations. In addition to many stone and bone tools, indicating grain-processing, spinning and weaving, the site is important for the evidence it has presented regarding metallurgy and trade.

Bronze was worked on the site, and fragments of crucibles and moulds were found, as well as actual bronze pins and brooches. Iron was also worked, and a smithy hearth is preserved in one of the outer buildings . Slag was found, but no iron artefacts. Sherds of Roman pottery and a bronze patera or ladle of Roman manufacture indicate at least indirect contact with the Romans.

Although Midhowe is an important site in terms of understanding Iron-Age industrial processes, it would be a mistake to assume that it was in any way a specialised industrial settlement, since similar small-scale activities are attested at most excavated broch sites, including Gurness. Such activities were inevitably associated with a degree of disposable wealth and patronage for craftsmen would have come from the leading members of society, presumably those whose families had organised the building of brochs.

Fragments of clay moulds provide evidence of bronze working at Midhowe. Iron, too, was smelted in an area outside the broch which was set aside as an industrial zone.

A Tour of Midhowe

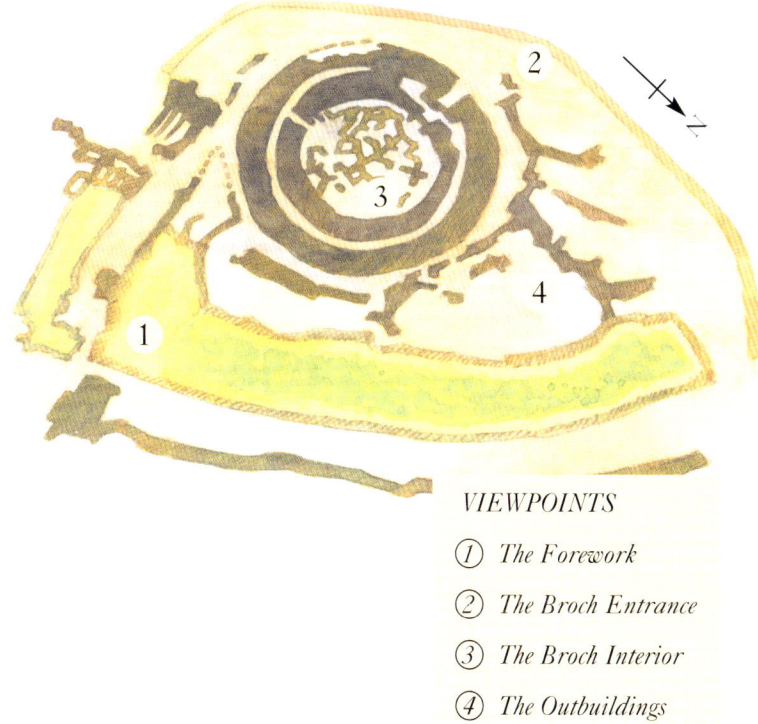

Midhowe from the air.

The site is approached by a path leading from the large modern building which houses the nearby chambered tomb, the 'howe' or burial mound which has given its name to the site. It is located on a narrow promontory between two steep-sided creeks or 'geos'. These may have provided a quarry for the building stone. The path approaches the broch along the original route: crossing the outer ditch by a causeway at its south-eastern end, it passes through the narrow entrance passage in the massive masonry 'forework' and emerges in the defended area. Ahead and to the right is the broch tower.

VIEWPOINTS

① *The Forework*

② *The Broch Entrance*

③ *The Broch Interior*

④ *The Outbuildings*

13

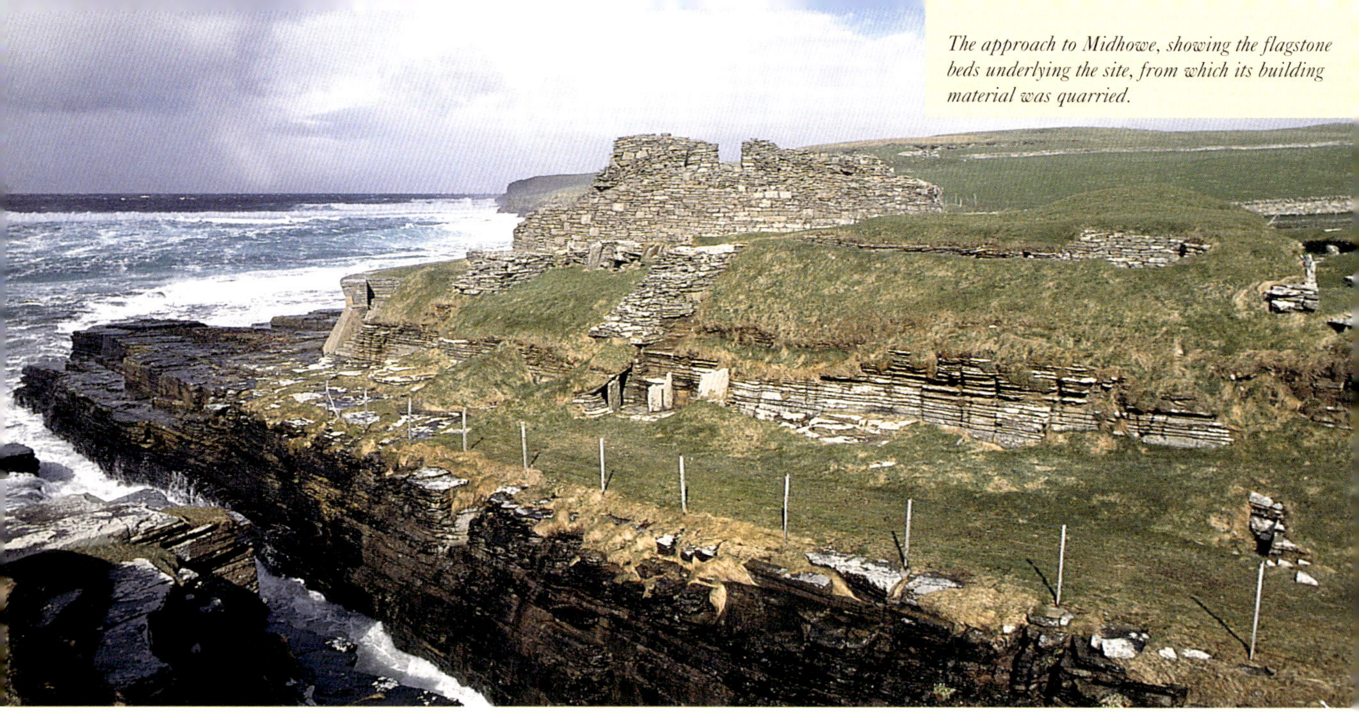

The approach to Midhowe, showing the flagstone beds underlying the site, from which its building material was quarried.

1 The Forework

The forework is clearly a defensive feature, perhaps a fighting platform on which defenders stationed themselves, hoping to dissuade attackers by a show of strength as much as by force of arms. On the back of this wall is a ledge which may have supported a lean-to timber structure. The narrow entrance passage was probably originally lintelled. The forework is built out into the inner edge of the outer ditch and the outer edge of the inner ditch, and it sits on the position of an earlier rampart, of slighter proportions.

The visitor should pause to note the partly infilled inner ditch and the traces of later buildings before circling round, clockwise, to the broch entrance.

2 The Broch Entrance

It is immediately apparent that the entrance to the broch tower does not align with the approach from the forework. It has been suggested that this is because the broch entrance faces the normal approach to the site, by sea, but it is more likely that this deliberate lack of alignment was a defensive feature, forcing any attacker who penetrated the forework line of defence to run around the foot of the broch tower before he could attempt the broch entrance. This 'defensive' layout is in contrast to the 'monumental' direct approach at Gurness.

The broch entrance is the usual narrow passage, with fittings for two doors and chambers in the wall on either side. Midhowe has a rather taller entrance passage than most brochs.

Outside the broch entrance at Midhowe. Vertically placed slabs against the wall to the far left appear to be buttressing for the unstable wall. The low chamber to the right of the entrance could have been a dog kennel, or perhaps a pig was kept there to eat food scraps: an early waste-disposal mechanism.

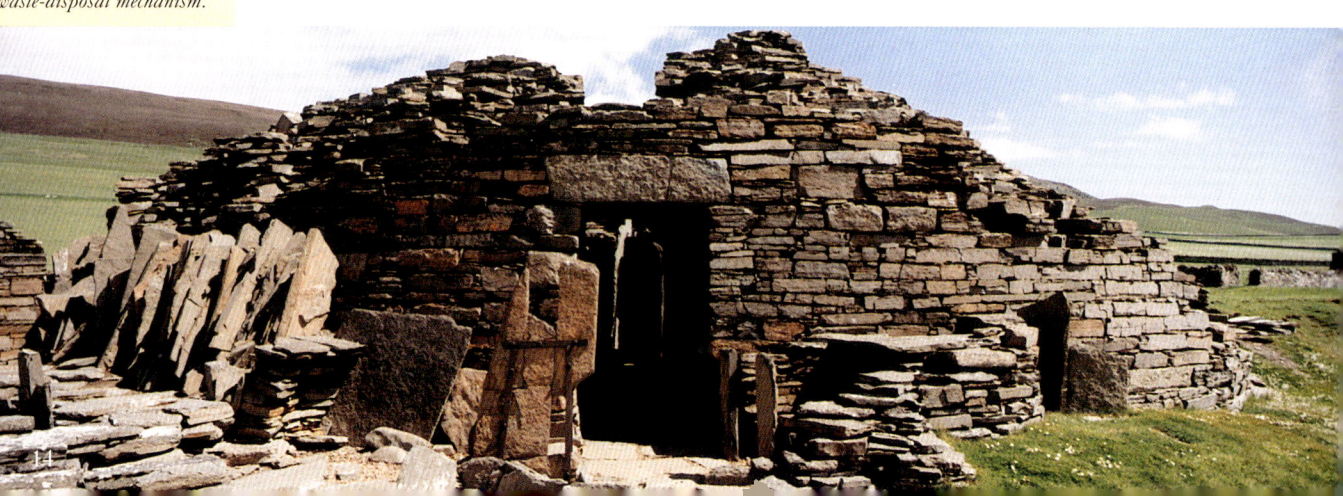

3   The Broch Interior

Within the broch are stone partitions, tanks and hearths, probably relating to secondary phases of occupation and almost certainly of several different periods. Particularly noteworthy is the fine spring-fed water tank in the floor and a hearth with sockets for what may have been a roasting spit.

The stair to the top of the broch is reached through a doorway in the inner face of the wall at head height. This was presumably once reached by a wooden stair or ladder. Like Gurness, Midhowe has suffered from partial collapse, the hollow walls sagging downwards and outwards soon after it was built. As at Gurness, the response was to fill the lower gallery level with tightly packed masonry and buttress the external walling. From the wall, which reaches 4.3 m above ground level, a fine view is obtained of the whole site.

When occupied, the interior would have been dark, as the whole structure would have been roofed by thatch or turf supported by stout timber posts. It may even have had a raised wooden floor below the roof, leaving the ground level free for cooking, storage and other domestic duties. A ledge which could have supported either such a floor or the outer ends of roofing timbers is visible on the inner wallface, 3.3 m from ground level. Alternatively, the stone partitions may themselves have supported an upper floor level.

The broch interior from the wallhead. The flagstone fittings on the floor divide it up into working and storage areas.

4   The Outbuildings

Leaving the broch, and moving again to the north, the visitor emerges into a group of low walls marking the position of several other buildings. In origin these seem to have been simply ancillary houses, like those at Gurness, but later in the site's history they were taken over for use as workshops. An iron-smelting hearth is preserved beneath a wood and glass cover. The best-preserved house is tucked between the broch and the back wall of the forework, and if there was a timber structure behind the forework, this must have been removed before the house was built.

The site tour may be concluded by climbing (carefully) onto the forework, to look down into the ditches and view the broch to advantage.

The Brochs of Scotland

By about 500 BC the Iron-Age inhabitants of Orkney had begun to build strong circular houses as the main dwellings of their farms. Gradually these became more sophisticated in design and formed the centres of small agricultural villages, frequently enclosed by outer defences in the form of ditches, banks or walls. There were also undefended settlements at this time, but these are less well studied: they are harder to locate than the massive brochs.

Brochs were imposing drystone structures, standing from 5 to 13 m high (the Broch of Mousa in Shetland still survives to a height of 13 m). Entrance was via a narrow passage through the wall, with a door part-way down, leading to an inner area usually about half the overall diameter.

From this area, openings gave access to chambers or 'cells' in or against the wall, and a doorway led to a stone staircase rising upwards within the wall thickness. This led up through a series of superimposed galleries, the floor of each forming the ceiling of the one below, emerging at the wallhead, which commanded a view of the village, the outer defences and the countryside beyond. Excavation evidence suggests that each broch may have had an inner structure of stone and wood. The surviving stone tower is to some extent merely a shell within which once sat the real dwelling place, possibly with one or more raised floors and covered by a thatched timber roof.

The Broch of Mousa in Shetland still stands to a height of over 13 metres.

Within the thickness of the wall of Mousa, the stairway leads to the top of the broch.

The brochs of the Northern Isles were impressive structures. However, they were often merely the central points of more complex settlements, sometimes of considerable extent. The precise role of the broch within the larger settlement is not established, but it would be reasonable to surmise that it was the residence of the principal family of the community, and probably also served as a gathering place for communal activities ranging from meeting for war to entertainment on winter evenings. It also provided the last defensive resort of the community.

In some parts of Scotland, brochs occur as isolated structures, without surrounding settlements or outer defences. This led to the theory that the 'broch villages', such as Gurness, were later accretions of houses around an original isolated tower. However, recent excavations at Howe, near Stromness, and re-examination of the evidence for earlier excavations at Gurness itself, now prompt archaeologists to believe that these larger settlements were intended from the outset, with the broch itself forming but part of a larger plan. It may be that the broch was a

building form which became particularly favoured and carried with it overtones of social status, so that brochs were built in a wide variety of circumstances, sometimes by small isolated groups and sometimes, as in much of Orkney, by relatively numerous and wealthy communities farming the best land. Brochs were widespread throughout northern and western Scotland and the Islands, but brochs with external houses and defences occur over a more restricted area, and brochs with sizeable villages outside seem to be peculiar to Orkney and northern Caithness.

By around 100 BC there were brochs standing or under construction in over 120 localities in Orkney, and throughout Scotland the number was well over 500.

Brochs, especially when surrounded by outer ramparts and ditches, were manifestly capable of being defended. The evidence for fighting or violent destruction of brochs is, however, almost non-existent. They probably indicate a society where mutual antagonisms, perhaps due to growing population and land shortages, and struggles over

The ground plans of the brochs of Gurness (left) and Midhowe (right).

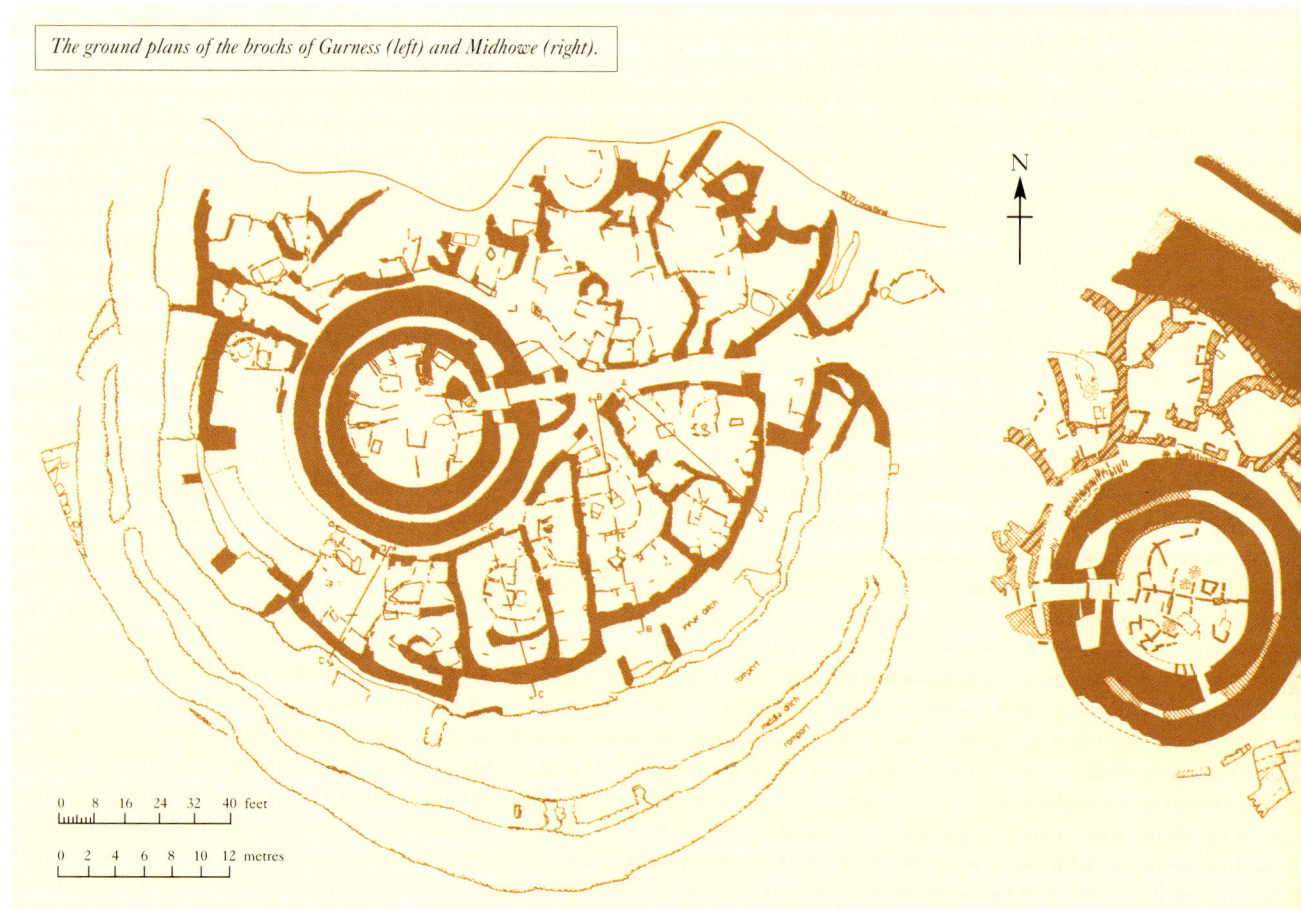

0   8   16   24   32   40 feet

0   2   4   6   8   10   12 metres

power and social status, were never far below the surface, but in which actual conflict seldom grew beyond local squabbles. The nature of brochs, with their essentially passive defensive arrangements, was neatly summed up by the anonymous thirteenth-century author of *Orkneyinga Saga*. Writing of the Broch of Mousa, which had been briefly re-occupied more than a thousand years after its construction, he wrote: 'it was an unhandy place to get at'. Brochs were by no means impregnable, given the available fighting techniques of the Iron Age in northern Scotland. But direct assault could be guaranteed to be costly of life, while prolonged siege was not an option, given the need to provide supplies for the encircling forces, who would have been relatively few in number, and given the probable threat from neighbours sympathetic to the plight of the besieged. So, by and large, brochs worked as a mutual deterrent. This conclusion is reinforced by the evidence from excavated sites which generally shows that broch settlements with outer ditches and walls tended to grow out over these defensive elements, rendering them useless for their original purpose.

As brochs became widespread, they probably became indicators of the importance of the leading families of each community, so that no group was felt to be of significance in society unless it had a broch at the heart of its lands. Over time, the symbolic function of brochs seems to have increased as the need for defence decreased. While fighting doubtless continued, the existence of a series of strong points tended to reduce the scope for the escalation of conflict beyond local brawls. The analogy with the many small medieval castles and tower-houses throughout Scotland is striking.

The coastal distribution of brochs shows how important sea and coastal travel must have been, even if we do not know what Iron-Age boats looked like. Contact with neighbours and farther afield must have been a regular occurrence to judge from the range of objects found on the settlement sites.

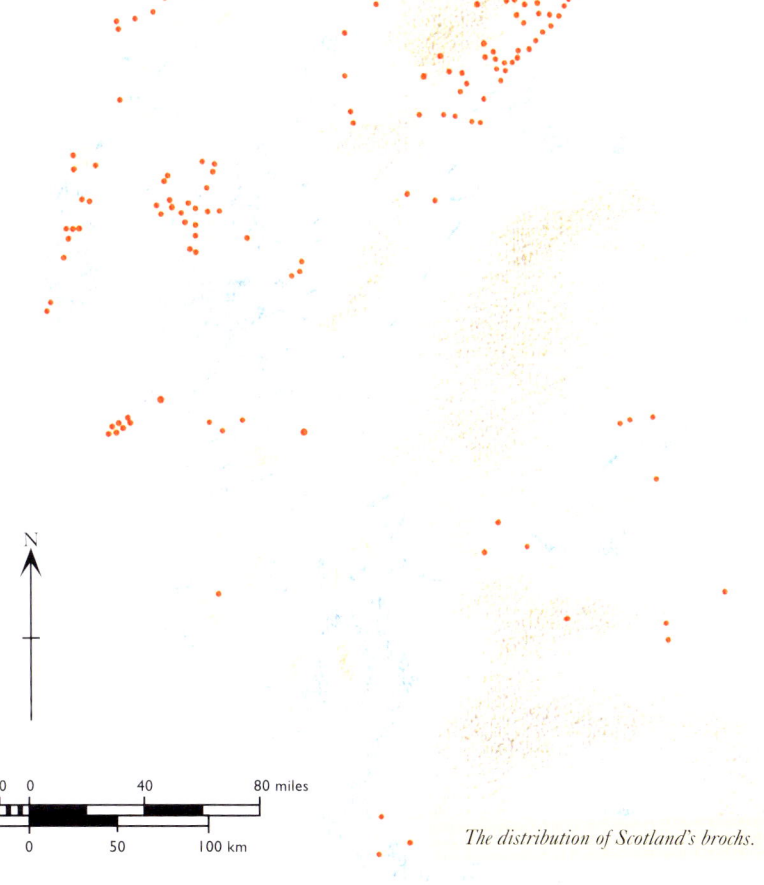

Midhowe
Gurness

The distribution of Scotland's brochs.

Artist's impression of the view across Eynhallow Sound from beside Gurness looking towards Midhowe. The sea and its shore would have been important for food and transport.

The Broch Builders

The people who built the brochs were farmers, successors to those who, many centuries before, had built the great chambered tombs of Orkney. Although they were in regular communication with other parts of Scotland, and perhaps ventured farther afield, there is no good evidence to suggest, as archaeologists once believed, that there was an invasion of 'broch-builders' from outside the region. However, the farmers of Iron-Age Orkney were, by the standards of northern Britain, prosperous and secure, with their mixed farming economy bolstered by the produce of the sea. They were probably well-connected, and trade or marriage would have brought fresh contacts, new ideas and innovative minds into the community. Orkney in the Iron Age was probably remarkably cosmopolitan.

Although considerable quantities of grain, mainly barley, were grown, farming was centred around the rearing of cattle, which provided meat, milk and leather. They may also have served as draught animals for ploughing. But more important, they represented wealth, and possession of cattle was probably the main index of social status, at least during the earlier Iron Age. There is some evidence that as time went on more 'modern' indicators of wealth also became current, for example exotic jewellery, but this remained subsidiary to the wealth 'on the hoof'. Sheep and goats were also kept, and spinning and weaving took place.

Pigs, hens and, possibly, geese were kept, and dogs were used for herding. Hunting, especially for red deer, seems to have been important, beyond the role merely of a pastime for those with leisure. Also important was wildfowling on the shores and marshes and the gathering of wild plants, seaweed and shellfish. Fishing from the shore and from skin-covered boats was also a vital component of the economy, with fish, seals and small whales all fair game.

Life would have been busy and work often hard, but starvation can seldom have been a likely spectre for the Iron-Age Orcadian. Long dark hours during the winter would have afforded time indoors to plan for the following season, weave and spin, tell tales and repair tools, fishing gear and boats. During the summer months much time would have been spent out of doors, with the late evenings perhaps enlivened by otter trapping along the shores or, for the more lawless spirits, forays to seek out and claim 'strayed' cattle. From such expeditions may have come the chief threat to what was a peaceful, settled, society: an image often lost to sight behind the misleading evidence of the many fortified brochs. It was almost certainly possible to live a normal lifetime in Iron-Age Orkney and never be involved in a fight to the death: the sea doubtless claimed more lives than did warfare; life was generally safe, solid, and routine.

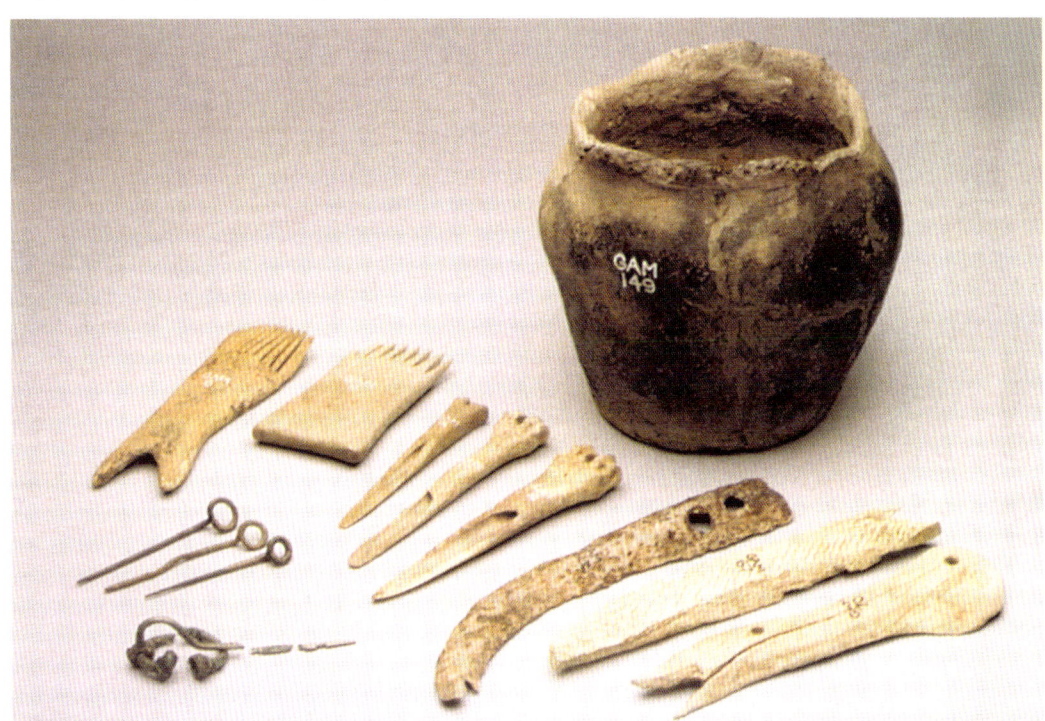

Iron-Age finds from Gurness: a typical pottery vessel, bronze pins and a penannular brooch, and a variety of bone artefacts. (Reproduced by kind permission of the National Museums of Scotland.)

After the Brochs

Gurness from the south-east. The 'Shamrock' house, the late Iron-Age or Pictish dwelling on display beside the Visitor Centre, originally stood immediately behind the wall in the left foreground.

Once the brochs ceased being built and used as defensive sites, the general picture is one of progressive abandonment, and a deterioration in the scale and quality of dwelling construction. Gurness is typical in illustrating a slow but irreversible trend away from monumental construction. It seems clear that brochs, originally conceived for reasons of defence, rapidly acquired connotations of social status. As the structure of society evolved in a way which ruled out forms of conflict in which brochs could play a useful role, so that they became functionally redundant, it was only a matter of time before they became socially irrelevant. The whole concept of 'monumentality', of showing power through building, seems to have foundered some time in the second or third century AD.

Where did the broch builders, or rather their descendants, go? Probably not very far. The pattern seems to be one of slow drift away from the nucleated settlements of the broch villages back to living in scattered farmsteads. There was probably also a social shift away from communal agriculture and (perhaps) joint ownership towards individual enterprise, once the nucleating force, the threat of attack, was perceived to have disappeared.

There is a possibility that there was a genuine reduction in population in Orkney between the broch period and the arrival of Viking settlers around AD 800. Archaeologists have had little success until recently in finding houses for the centuries immediately preceding the Viking settlement, but now examples are known around Birsay, on Sanday and Papa Westray and at Skaill in East Mainland. These, along with the 'Shamrock' house at Gurness (see page 6), suggest that there was a substantial, dispersed settlement pattern. A further possibility is that as dispersion got under way the population also began to build in turf and/or timber (although the latter would have had to be imported), and it may be that buildings of considerable quality were constructed in these perishable materials and have

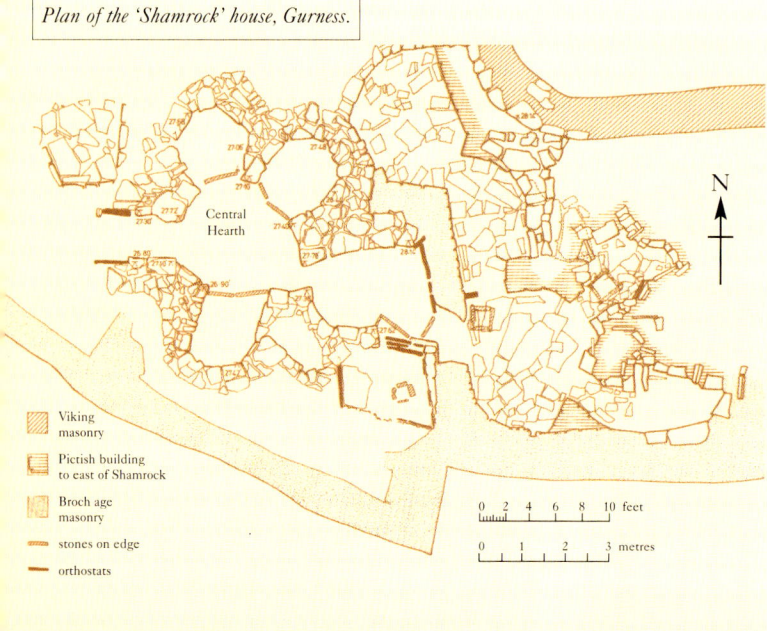

Plan of the 'Shamrock' house, Gurness.

Central Hearth

Viking masonry

Pictish building to east of Shamrock

Broch age masonry

stones on edge

orthostats

N

0 2 4 6 8 10 feet

0 1 2 3 metres

not survived. Indeed, it could well be that a building of imported timber may have been more of a status symbol, an indicator of conspicuous consumption, than a broch built of local stone. So far, we do not have the evidence to decide one way or the other.

The period after the brochs, then, represents a gap in knowledge when compared to the well-studied broch period. There are increasing numbers of settlement sites known. We know from documentary sources that Orkney was either part of, or allied with, the Pictish kingdom whose heartland lay in mainland eastern Scotland. Carved stones and Pictish writings, 'oghams', support this. The precise relationship with Pictland remains obscure, but Orkney's agricultural wealth suggests it is unlikely to have been a peripheral component of any political or economic grouping of which it was a member.

A Viking Graveyard?

The Vikings who settled in Orkney from around AD 800 often used the mounds of earlier settlement sites as burial places, and this was the case at Gurness. In the ninth or tenth centuries, before they were Christianised, these pagans (who originally came from Norway) buried their dead with grave-goods to accompany them to the next world. Although only one complete grave was found at Gurness, the excavators found human bones and other Viking objects elsewhere. This suggests that other Vikings were buried here as well.

The one complete grave was that of a woman. The grave-goods that accompanied her included a sickle blade and a pair of 'tortoise' brooches (see below). The finds from elsewhere on the site include shield bosses, the type of object buried with Viking men.

A stone bearing roughly executed Pictish symbols, from Gurness. Such designs, dating from the sixth, seventh and eighth centuries AD, are widespread in north and east Scotland, but their precise meaning is not known.

Excavating the Viking grave, 1930s' style.

Further Reading

I Armit *Celtic Scotland* (1997)

J G Callander & W G Grant 'The broch of Midhowe, Rousay, Orkney'. *Proc Soc Antiq Scot* 68 (1933–4), 444–516.

J W Hedges *Bu, Gurness and the Brochs of Orkney* (3 vols) (1987)

A C Renfrew *The Prehistory of Orkney 4000BC–1000AD* (1990)

A Ritchie *Exploring Scotland's Heritage: Orkney* (1996)

A Ritchie *Scotland BC* (1999)

A Ritchie *Picts* (1999)

A Ritchie and D J Breeze *Invaders of Scotland* (2000)

G Ritchie *The Brochs of Scotland* (1988)

Midhowe Broch from the north-west. (Copyright Richard Welsby.)